398.2   Richardson, I. M.
R   Odysseus and the
              great challenge

Odysseus and the Great Challenge

Tales from the Odyssey

Written by I. M. Richardson
Illustrated by Hal Frenck

Troll Associates

Library of Congress Cataloging in Publication Data

Richardson, I. M.
  Odysseus and the great challenge.

  (Tales from the Odyssey / adapted by I. M. Richardson;
bk. 5)
  Summary: His listeners hear of Odysseus's near-tragic
encounters with the Sirens, with Charybdis the whirlpool,
with the six-headed monster Scylla, and with the sun god
Helios.
  [1. Mythology, Greek] I. Frenck, Hal, ill.
II. Homer. Odyssey. III. Series: Richardson, I. M.
Tales from the Odyssey; bk. 5. IV. Title.
PZ8.1.R396Tal 1984 bk. 5 292'.13s [292'.13] 83-14232
ISBN 0-8167-0013-3 (lib. bdg.)
ISBN 0-8167-0014-1 (pbk.)

"Tell us how you lost your ship," said the king. "Was it in a storm?" asked the queen. "Did Poseidon, god of the sea, wreck your vessel and drown your men?" And Odysseus replied, "No. My men brought the trouble upon themselves."

Odysseus was King of Ithaca and hero of the Trojan War. He had left Troy nearly ten years ago. But Poseidon had sent one misfortune after another to keep Odysseus from returning home. At last, he had been washed ashore on a friendly island. The king and queen had promised to send him home. "Tell us what happened," they said.

"When we left the island of the goddess Circe," said Odysseus, "I knew we would have to pass the Singing Sirens. They use their sweet voices to lure passing sailors to certain death. The rocky island on which they live is littered with bones. They are the bones of sailors who dared to listen to the Sirens' lovely songs.

"Before we came within earshot of the Sirens, I told my men what I planned to do. 'I will make plugs for your ears,' I said, 'so you will not hear the Sirens' songs. I alone will listen to their sweet voices. But you must tie me to the mast of the ship until we have safely passed the island.'

"I warned them that they were not to untie me, no matter what happened. Suddenly, the wind died. The men dropped the sails and took out the oars. I chopped a huge ball of wax into small pieces. Then I went from man to man, plugging their ears so they could not hear. Finally, they tied me to the mast.

"The Sirens saw our ship, and sang out. Their voices were like the sweetest music, and I longed to go to them. I ordered my men to change course, and steer for the island, but of course, they did not hear me. Then I began shouting and struggling to free myself from the ropes that bound me.

"My efforts, however, were all in vain. When my crew saw me struggling, two men put down their oars and tied me even more tightly than before. Then they returned to their places and took up their oars again. They could not hear the lovely refrains that tortured me and drove me mad with longing.

"At length, my men untied me and removed the wax plugs from their ears. We were far away from the island, and I could no longer hear the Sirens' voices. But ahead lay a new danger. I could see the mist hanging above Charybdis. Charybdis was a terrible whirlpool that dragged ships down to the bottom of the sea, then spouted them up in shattered bits and pieces.

"As we drew closer, there was a loud roaring noise. Charybdis was spouting. My men dropped their oars and trembled in fear. I walked among them, speaking brave words designed to lift their spirits. 'We have survived many great dangers,' I said. 'This is but one more test of our courage.' Fortunately, I had a plan.

"Ahead of us lay a narrow strait. The whirlpool was at the base of a low cliff at one side of the strait. I knew we could not battle Charybdis and win. So I said, 'We must keep to the other side of the strait, and row with all our strength.' At the other side of the strait was a smooth rock wall. About halfway up its side was a dark and gloomy cave.

"I dared not tell my men about the terror that hid inside that cave. Scylla was its name, and it was a horrible monster. It had twelve legs. Its six heads were on long, snake-like necks that could reach down to any passing ship. Each time a ship went by, Scylla would grab six sailors—and eat them!

"As my men leaned into their oars, I took out my armor and put it on. I had been warned that no mortal could fight against Scylla and win, but I prepared for battle anyway. With a spear in each hand, I stood at the bow of the ship. I kept a sharp watch for any movement that might be the six-headed monster.

"But I saw no sign of Scylla. We passed into the strait, staying as far from Charybdis as we could. Still, we were close enough to feel the suction as the whirlpool swallowed the salty sea. We could see the swirling waters spinning down and around, racing toward the deep, sandy bottom.

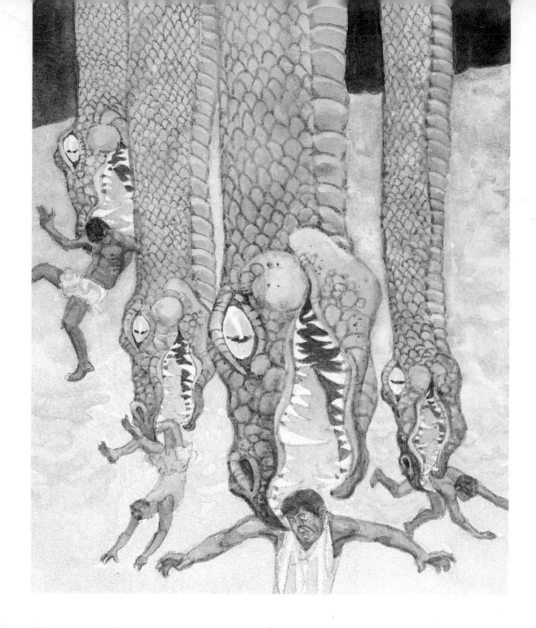

"We trembled as we watched the terror of the whirlpool. At that very moment, Scylla reached down from the cave on the other side of the ship and snatched six of my best men. I spun around when I heard their cries, but it was already too late. Scylla had already hoisted them up out of reach.

"My unfortunate companions screamed and moaned as the monster pulled them into the darkened cave. There Scylla ate them, one by one. I could do nothing but urge my men to row faster. I feared that if we did not get through the strait before Scylla had finished, the monster would reach out and seize six more of us!

'We did not rest until the twin terrors of Scylla and Charybdis lay far behind us. Next, we approached the island of the sun god, Helios. A prophet had warned me about this place. 'If you wish to reach home,' he had said, 'do not harm the cattle of the sun god.' Even now, I could hear the sounds of the cattle echoing up from the grassy pastures.

"'This island looks inviting,' I said, 'but we must not stop here.' At once, my men began to grumble and complain. Finally, I agreed to let them go ashore for the night. First, however, I made them promise not to harm the cattle. They agreed at once, and we headed for shore.

"After a good supper on the sandy beach, I chose one of the crew members to stand watch, and the rest of us fell into a deep and restful sleep. But during the night, a storm began to brew. Clouds blew in from the south and covered the stars.

"By morning, the winds were blowing in a fury. We moved up from the beach and found shelter inside a cave. 'Since we have plenty of food,' I said, 'there is no reason to harm the cattle. They belong to the sun god, who sees everything.' My men again vowed not to touch the sun god's cattle.

'The howling wind did not let up for a month. By then, we had eaten all the food we had brought from the ship. Now we had to hunt and fish for our meals, and we were not having much luck. One day, I went off by myself to ask the gods if they would smile upon us. Instead, they sent down a great weariness upon me.

"While I slept, one of my men gathered the others together and said, 'We are slowly starving. I say we take some of these cattle and make a feast of them. If the gods should strike us dead, at least that is better than dying a slow death by starvation.' The others quickly agreed.

"Then they went off and brought back several of the sun god's cattle. After they had made the proper offerings to the gods, they built a roaring fire. Finally, they put the steaks on spits, so they could cook them. As soon as I awoke, I smelled the roasting meat and knew what had happened.

"The sun god also knew what happened, and he was furious. He cried out to Zeus, saying, 'Strike them down, Father Zeus! If the mortals guilty of this crime are not punished, I will go down to the Underworld and light up the Kingdom of the Dead.' And Zeus promised that the guilty would not go unpunished.

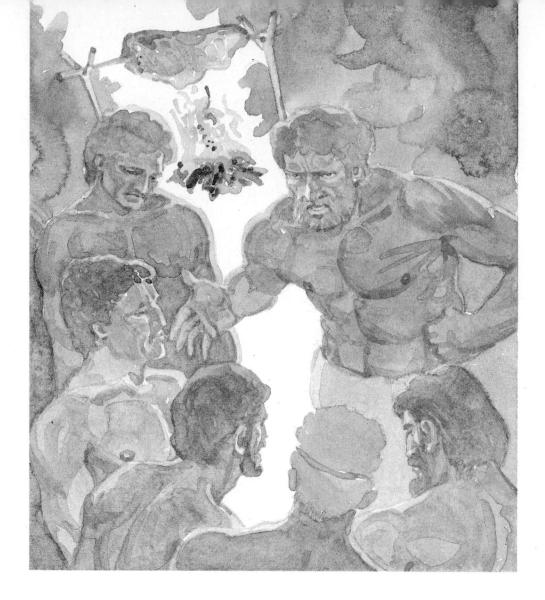

"As soon as I returned to the camp, I cried out, 'Have you all gone mad? Your reckless behavior will bring the wrath of the gods upon us!' But it was already too late. Indeed, as the meat began roasting on the fire, the empty skins of the cattle crawled away by themselves, and ghostly sounds began to haunt us.

"As you might imagine, the crew was eager to leave that place. So when the next favorable wind began to blow, we boarded our ship and rowed out into deep water. The breeze filled the sails, and we put some distance between us and the island of the sun god. Before long, we were surrounded by nothing but endless sea.

"Suddenly, a black cloud came and hung above the ship. Then a furious tempest ripped through the sails, splitting the mast and sending the rigging into the sea. Zeus shot a thunderbolt straight into the hull, hurling the men overboard. That was how he punished them for eating the sun god's cattle. I never saw them again.

"I stayed with the ship until the waves tore it apart. Finally, I grabbed a piece of the mast, and lashed it to the wooden keel. On this makeshift raft, I drifted with the wind. But the wind had changed, and by morning, I had been blown back to those twin terrors—Scylla and Charybdis.

"Just as the whirlpool began pulling me down, I reached up above me. I seized the branch of a fig tree that grew out from the side of the cliff. There I hung, watching as the mast and keel were swallowed. All I could do was hope that Charybdis would spout them up again before I lost my grip on the branch.

"At the last moment, the whirlpool spouted, and up came my mast and keel. I let go of the branch and dropped into the water next to them. Then I climbed on, and paddled away as fast as I could. Scylla did not see me. I never would have escaped had the monster noticed me in the strait.

"Ten days later, I reached Calypso's island," concluded Odysseus. "I was held there for seven years. But finally I built a raft and sailed away. The raft was lost in a storm, and I was washed up on your shores." To this the king and queen replied, "Tomorrow we shall send you to your homeland." Odysseus smiled at the thought. He was finally going home to Ithaca!